# Contents

Some words are shown in bold, **like this**. You can find out what they mean by looking in the glossary.

# Meet the silkworms

A silkworm is not a worm.
It is a caterpillar.

A silkworm is an **insect**. It looks like it has many legs, but only six are true legs. It uses the other ten legs to cling to plants.

1 day

3 weeks

5-7 weeks

**LIFE CYCLE OF A...**

# Silkworm

## Revised and Updated

Ron Fridell
and
Patricia Walsh

**www.heinemannlibrary.co.uk**
Visit our website to find out more information about Heinemann Library books.

**To order:**
☎ Phone +44 (0) 1865 888066
🖹 Fax +44 (0) 1865 314091
🖥 Visit www.heinemannlibrary.co.uk

Edited by Adrian Vigliano, Harriet Milles, and Diyan Leake
Designed by Kimberly R. Miracle and Tony Miracle
Original illustrations ©Capstone Global Library Limited 1998, 2009
Illustrated by David Westerfield
Picture research by Tracy Cummins and Heather Mauldin
Originated by Chroma Graphics (Overseas) Pte. Ltd.
Printed in China by South China Printing Company Ltd.

ISBN 978 0431 99955 5 (hardback)
13 12 11 10 09
10 9 8 7 6 5 4 3 2 1

ISBN 978 0431 99973 9 (paperback)
13 12 11 10 09
10 9 8 7 6 5 4 3 2 1

**British Library Cataloguing in Publication Data**
Fridell, Ron.
   Life cycle of a silkworm. -- 2nd ed.
   1. Silkworms--Life cycles--Juvenile literature.
   I. Title II. Silkworm III. Walsh, Patricia, 1951-
   595.7'8156-dc22
A full catalogue record for this book is available from the British Library.

**Acknowledgements**
We would like to thank the following for permission to reproduce photographs: ©Em Ahart pp. **12**, **21**; Corbis pp. **14**, **15**, **28 bottom** (©Gallo Images/Anthony Bannister), **26** (©Wolfgang Kaehler); Getty Images pp. **10**, **28 top right** (©Keren Su), **24** (©Dennis Johnson); ©James Kalisch p. **29 top right**; ©Dwight Kuhn pp. **6**, **8**, **16**, **19**, **28 top left**, **29 top left**; Photolibrary pp. **20**, **29 bottom** (©Paul Beard)Photo Researchers Inc. p. **23** (©S. Nagendra); Photoshot pp. **7**, **13**, **22**, (©Bruce Coleman/E.R. Degginger); Shutterstock pp. **5** (©July Flower), **11** (©sf2301420max), **25** (©Joris Van Den Heuvel) **27** (©Naomi Hasegawa); University of Nebraska pp. **4**, **9**, **17**, **18** (©James Kalisch).

Cover photograph of a silkworm reproduced with permission of age fotostock (©San Rostro).

We would like to thank Michael Bright for his invaluable help in the preparation of this book.

Every effort has been made to contact copyright holders of material reproduced in this book. Any omissions will be rectified in subsequent printings if notice is given to the publisher.

Many years ago, silkworms lived in the wild. Today, most silkworms are **domesticated**. They live only on silk farms.

Silk farmers **breed** silkworms to get the silk thread they make.

**8 weeks**

**10 weeks**

**11 weeks**

# Egg

The female silk moth lays hundreds of eggs.

The silkworm begins life in a tiny egg. The egg is one of about 300 sticky, yellow eggs laid by the female silk **moth**.

1 day

3 weeks

5-7 weeks

The egg needs to stay cold for a few weeks. Then the egg is warmed up and its centre turns black.

Once the egg is warm, it takes about ten days to **hatch**.

8 weeks

10 weeks

11 weeks

# Hatching

The little black larva has hatched out of the egg.

When the tiny silkworm **larva** is ready to **hatch**, it bites a hole in the egg. Then it wriggles out.

1 day

3 weeks

5-7 weeks

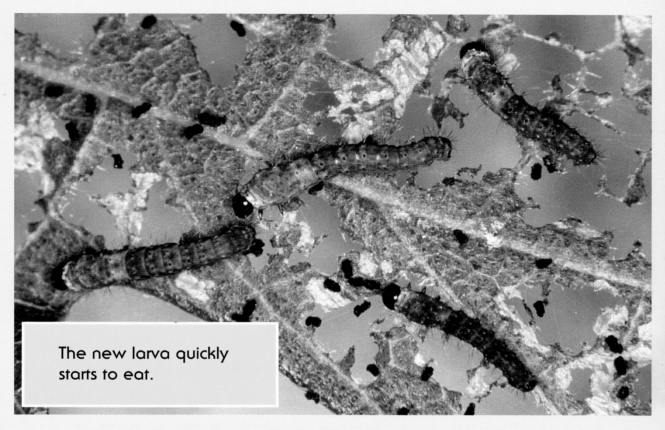

The new larva quickly starts to eat.

The newly hatched silkworm larva looks like a tiny black string. At first it is too weak to crawl very far, but it is ready to eat.

8 weeks

10 weeks

11 weeks

# Larva

The new **larva** needs to have its food close by. In a few days, the larva will be stronger. It will crawl from leaf to leaf.

The larva eats only mulberry tree leaves.

1 day

3 weeks

5-7 weeks

The larva has changed from black to white.

The larva eats a lot of mulberry leaves. It does not drink water. It gets enough **moisture** from the leaves.

8 weeks

10 weeks

11 weeks

# Moulting

You can see this silkworm larva wriggling out of its old skin.

The **larva's** skin does not stretch as it grows. To get bigger, a silkworm must **moult**. The old skin splits. The silkworm wriggles out wearing its new skin.

1 day

3 weeks

5-7 weeks

The silkworm larva grows to be about as long as your finger.

The larva moults four times. After the fourth moult, the larva eats even more mulberry leaves than it did before.

8 weeks

10 weeks

11 weeks

# Spinning the cocoon

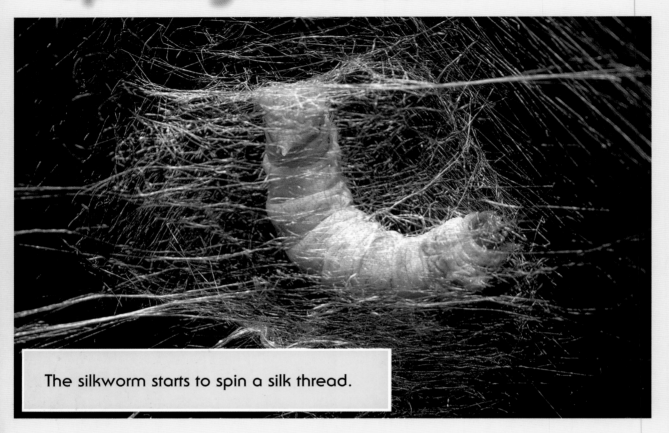

The silkworm starts to spin a silk thread.

The **larva** is ready to spin a **cocoon**. It makes its cocoon from one long, sticky silk thread that comes from its mouth.

1 day

3 weeks

5-7 weeks

The silkworm takes about three to four days to spin its cocoon.

First the larva spins a silk web. Then it spins and spins for three days. It spins a silk cocoon around itself.

8 weeks

10 weeks

11 weeks

# Pupa

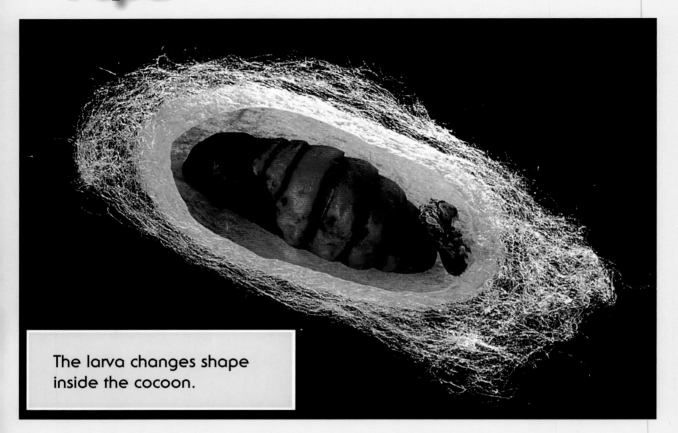

The larva changes shape inside the cocoon.

Inside the **cocoon**, the **larva moults** one last time. This time it changes to a brown **pupa** with a hard shell.

1 day

3 weeks

5-7 weeks

It is time for the moth to leave the cocoon.

After two weeks the shell splits. The pupa has turned into a silk **moth**. The moth spits a special liquid. The liquid wets the inside of the cocoon, and makes a hole.

8 weeks

10 weeks

11 weeks

# Leaving the cocoon

The moth looks very different from the silkworm it used to be.

The **pupa** has changed into a white adult silk **moth.** The moth has wings and large eyes. On its head there are two **antennae** that look like feathers.

1 day

3 weeks

5-7 weeks

The silk moth dries itself on the cocoon.

The silk moth pulls itself right through the hole in the cocoon. In about an hour, its damp wings unfold and dry.

8 weeks

10 weeks

11 weeks

# Silk moth

The silk **moth** has six legs and two **antennae**. It also has four wings. But a **domesticated** moth cannot fly.

The silk moth is about 3–5 centimetres (2 inches) wide.

1 day

3 weeks

5-7 weeks

The silk moth can only flutter and hop about.

For the next few days, the silk moth does not eat or drink anything.

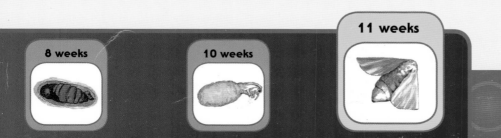

8 weeks

10 weeks

11 weeks

# Mating

Soon after coming out of the **cocoon**, the female **moth** gives off a **scent**. This helps a male moth to find her. Then they **mate**.

The female silk moth is bigger than the male.

1 day

3 weeks

5-7 weeks

The female silk moth lays her eggs a few hours after mating.

After mating, the male moth dies. When the female moth has laid her eggs, she will die, too.

8 weeks

10 weeks

11 weeks

# Silk from silkworms

These silkworms are busy spinning their cocoons.

Silk farmers **breed** silkworms for their cocoons. The silk thread of the **cocoons** is woven into silk cloth.

1 day

3 weeks

5-7 weeks

Cocoons with holes are not good for making silk cloth.

On silk farms, most **pupas** never change into **moths**. If moths were allowed to come out of the cocoons, there would be holes in the cocoons.

8 weeks

10 weeks

11 weeks

# Making silk cloth

Machines twist the threads together to make **strands** of silk.

The long, white, silk thread from the **cocoon** is as thin as a spiderweb. It is unwound from the cocoon.

1 day

3 weeks

5-7 weeks

The strands of silk are woven into silk cloth. The cloth can be **dyed** any colour to make beautiful clothes.

These girls are wearing dresses made of silk cloth.

# Life cycle

Egg

Larva

Cocoon

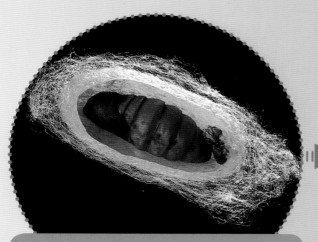

Pupa

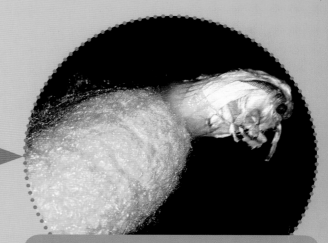

Leaving the cocoon

Silk moth

# Fact file

- The silkworm **larva** moves its head backwards and forwards in a figure-of-eight pattern as it spins its **cocoon**.

- It takes 110 cocoons to make a silk tie. It takes 630 cocoons to make a silk shirt.

- Other kinds of **moths** can fly to escape **predators**. A **domesticated** silk moth has no predators, so it does not fly.

- A single thread of silk from a silkworm's cocoon can be one mile long. That is about as long as 17 football pitches laid end to end.

- A single thread of silk is stronger than the same size thread of some types of steel.

# Glossary

**antenna**  long, thin feeler on an insect's head. (More than one are called antennae.)

**cocoon**  silken case that protects the pupa inside it

**breed**  to care for an animal or plant until it is fully grown

**domesticated**  cared for by humans

**dye**  change the colour of fabric

**hatch**  come out of an egg

**insect**  small animal that has six legs, a body with three parts, and wings

**larva**  caterpillar-like stage of an insect's life when it eats and grows

**mate**  when a male and female come together to make babies

**moisture**  water, wetness

**moth**  insect with a thick body and four wide wings. A moth is similar to a butterfly.

**moult**  shed the outer skin

**predator**  animal that eats other animals

**pupa**  resting stage in an insect's life, between larva and adult

**scent**  odour or smell

**strand**  thread or string

# More books to read

*How We Use: Silk,* Chris Oxlade (Raintree, 2005)

*Investigate: Life Cycles,* Charlotte Guillain and
Sue Barraclough (Heinemann Library, 2008)

# Index